Monster Vehicles

BY DEREK ZOBEL

BELLWETHER MEDIA • MINNEAPOLIS, MN

TORQUE ™

Are you ready to take it to the extreme? Torque books thrust you into the action-packed world of sports, vehicles, and adventure. These books may include dirt, smoke, fire, and dangerous stunts.

WARNING: READ AT YOUR OWN RISK.

This edition first published in 2008 by Bellwether Media.

No part of this publication may be reproduced in whole or in part without written permission of the publisher. For information regarding permission, write to Bellwether Media Inc., Attention: Permissions Department, Post Office Box 19349, Minneapolis, MN 55419.

Library of Congress Cataloging-in-Publication Data

Zobel, Derek, 1983-
  Monster vehicles / by Derek Zobel.
      p. cm. -- (Torque--cool rides)
  Summary: "Full color photography accompanies engaging information about Monster vehicles. The combination of high-interest subject matter and light text is intended for students in grades 3 through 7"--Provided by publisher.
  Includes bibliographical references and index.
  ISBN-13: 978-1-60014-151-5 (hardcover : alk. paper)
  ISBN-10: 1-60014-151-X (hardcover : alk. paper)
  1. Monster trucks--Juvenile literature. I. Title.

TL230.15.Z63 2008
629.224--dc22

2007040565

Contents

What Are Monster Vehicles?

Fans cheer as a monster truck speeds toward a line of cars. The monster truck hits a small jump and launches into the air. It crashes down onto the cars, crushing them beneath its huge tires.

Monster vehicles are custom-built machines with huge tires. The most popular monster vehicles are monster trucks. They compete in thrilling races and freestyle events for fans all over the world.

Fast FaCt

On September 11th, 1999, Dan Runte set the world monster truck long-jump record in Bigfoot 14 in Smyrna, Tennessee. He jumped the truck a distance of 202 feet, clearing a Boeing 727 jetliner.

Monster Vehicle History

The first monster vehicle was built by a man named Bob Chandler in the 1970s. He made the **chassis** of his 1974 Ford F-250 pickup truck bigger and stronger. He also added 66-inch (167-centimeter) tires. He called his creation Bigfoot.

People enjoyed watching Bigfoot crush cars. Many people who saw Bigfoot wanted to build monster vehicles of their own. They began building monster trucks, cars, vans, and motorcycles.

Fast Fact

A monster truck's engine usually has between 1200 and 1500 horsepower. That's about six times the power of a normal car!

11

Monster Vehicle Parts

People who build monster vehicles need to make them powerful and light. They also need to make them strong.

Racers who want to increase the speed of their monster vehicle can add a bigger engine. They can also use a light chassis so the truck weighs less. Monster vehicles need to have tough **suspension systems** and strong **axles** for jumping. They also need to be **durable** to handle rough **terrain**.

The **body** of a monster vehicle is another important feature. Drivers sit in the body. Some monster vehicles use bodies from normal vehicles. Other monster vehicles have custom-built bodies.

Fast Fact
The biggest tires ever used on a monster truck were 10 feet (3 meters) tall!

The weight of a monster vehicle's body is important for speed. Originally, the bodies of all monster vehicles were made of metal. Now some are made of **fiberglass**. Fiberglass is just as strong as some metals, but weighs much less. Monster vehicles with fiberglass bodies can go faster than those made from metals.

Many monster vehicles have custom paint jobs. Most monster vehicles have a rough and tough style. Flames, lightning bolts, sharp teeth, and claws are all common designs. Some owners may even give their monster vehicle a tough name.

Monster Vehicles in Action

The first monster vehicle competitions were for monster trucks. They remain the most popular today. An exciting part of monster truck events is racing. Monster truck racetracks are filled with obstacles. In order to win, drivers must be able to accelerate quickly, turn sharply, and jump cars.

Fast Fact

Robosaurus can crush cars with its hands or jaws. It can also shoot 20-foot (6-meter) flames out of its nose!

Some competitions also include freestyle events. Drivers have a set amount of time to perform as many tricks as possible. They go over jumps and do tricks such as **slap wheelies** and **donuts.** The driver who gets the loudest cheers from the crowd wins the event.

A few events feature special kinds of monster vehicles. They do not race or perform tricks. They are simply for show. One such monster vehicle is a 40-foot (12-meter) tall car-destroying monster vehicle called Robosaurus!

Glossary

axle–a rod in the center of a wheel; the wheel spins around the axle.

body–the part of a vehicle that carries the passengers

chassis–the metal tubing that forms the frame of the car; the chassis supports the body of a monster vehicle.

donut–a trick in which a monster truck spins in circles

durable–strong and long-lasting

fiberglass–a strong material made from glass fibers

slap wheelie–a trick in which a monster truck lands and its front wheels slap the ground and bounce into the air

suspension system–a series of springs and shock absorbers that connect the chassis of a monster vehicle to its wheels

terrain– the natural surface features of the land

To Learn More

AT THE LIBRARY

Brubaker, Ken. *Monster Trucks*. Osceola, Wisc.: Motorbooks, 2003.

Levete, Sarah. *Monster Trucks*. Vero Beach, Fla.: Rourke, 2005.

Nelson, Kristin L. *Monster Trucks*. Minneapolis, Minn.: Lerner, 2002.

ON THE WEB

Learning more about monster vehicles is as easy as 1, 2, 3.

1. Go to www.factsurfer.com

2. Enter "monster vehicles" into search box.

3. Click the "Surf" button and you will see a list of related web sites.

With factsurfer.com, finding more information is just a click away.

Index

4/19 (58) 6/19